TRUTH OVER LIES

LOVEGODGREATLY.COM

Printed in the United States of America

Library of Congress Cataloging-in-Publication Data

Printed in the United States of America

23 22 21 20 19 18

6   5   4   3   2   1

**AT LOVE GOD GREATLY, YOU'LL FIND
REAL, AUTHENTIC WOMEN. WOMEN WHO
ARE IMPERFECT, YET FORGIVEN.**

Women who desire less of us, and a whole lot
more of Jesus. Women who long to know God
through His Word, because we know that Truth
transforms and sets us free. Women who are
better together, saturated in God's Word and in
community with one another.

Welcome, friend. We're so glad you're here...

CONTENTS

WELCOME

We are glad you have decided to join us in this Bible study! First of all, please know that you have been prayed for! It is not a coincidence you are participating in this study.

Our prayer for you is simple: that you will grow closer to our Lord as you dig into His Word each and every day! As you develop the discipline of being in God's Word on a daily basis, our prayer is that you will fall in love with Him even more as you spend time reading from the Bible.

Each day before you read the assigned Scripture(s), pray and ask God to help you understand it. Invite Him to speak to you through His Word. Then listen. It's His job to speak to you, and it's your job to listen and obey.

As you go through this study, join us in the following resources below:

Take time to read the verses over and over again. We are told in Proverbs to search and you will find: "Search for it like silver, and hunt for it like hidden treasure. Then you will understand" (Prov. 2:4–5 NCV).

Weekly Blog Posts •

Weekly Memory Verses •

Weekly Challenges •

Facebook, Twitter, Instagram •

LoveGodGreatly.com •

Hashtags: #LoveGodGreatly •

All of us here at Love God Greatly can't wait for you to get started, and we hope to see you at the finish line. Endure, persevere, press on—and don't give up! Finish well what you are beginning today. We will be here every step of the way, cheering you on! We are in this together. Fight to rise early, to push back the stress of the day, to sit alone and spend time in God's Word! Let's see what God has in store for you in this study! Journey with us as we learn to love God greatly with our lives!

RESOURCES

Join Us

ONLINE
lovegodgreatly.com

STORE
lovegodgreatly.com/store

FACEBOOK
facebook.com/LoveGodGreatly

INSTAGRAM
instagram.com/lovegodgreatlyofficial

TWITTER
@_LoveGodGreatly

DOWNLOAD THE APP

CONTACT US
info@lovegodgreatly.com

CONNECT
#LoveGodGreatly

LOVE
GOD
GREATLY

Love God Greatly (LGG) is a beautiful community of women who use a variety of technology platforms to keep each other accountable in God's Word. We start with a simple Bible reading plan, but it doesn't stop there.

Some women gather in homes and churches locally, while others connect online with women across the globe. Whatever the method, we lovingly lock arms and unite for this purpose: to love God greatly with our lives.

Would you consider reaching out and doing this study with someone?

In today's fast-paced technology-driven world, it would be easy to study God's Word in an isolated environment that lacks encouragement or support, but that isn't the intention here at Love God Greatly. God created us to live in community with Him and with those around us.

We need each other, and we live life better together. Because of this, would you consider reaching out and doing this study with someone?

Rest assured we'll be studying right alongside you—learning with you, cheering for you, enjoying sweet fellowship, and smiling from ear to ear as we watch God unite women together—intentionally connecting hearts and minds for His glory.

So here's the challenge: call your mom, your sister, your grandma, the girl across the street, or the college friend across the country. Gather a group of girls from your church or workplace, or meet in a coffee shop with friends you have always wished you knew better.

Arm-in-arm and hand-in-hand, let's do this thing…together.

SOAP STUDY
HOW AND WHY TO SOAP

In this study we offer you a study journal to accompany the verses we are reading. This journal is designed to help you interact with God's Word and learn to dig deeper, encouraging you to slow down and reflect on what God is saying to you that day.

At Love God Greatly, we use the SOAP Bible study method. Before beginning, let's take a moment to define this method and share why we recommend using it during your quiet time in the following pages.

It's one thing to simply read Scripture. But when you interact with it, intentionally slowing down to really reflect on it, suddenly words start popping off the page. The SOAP method allows you to dig deeper into Scripture and see more than you would if you simply read the verses and then went on your merry way.

The most important ingredients in the SOAP method are your interaction with God's Word and your application of His Word to your life.

The most important ingredients in the SOAP method are your interaction with God's Word and your application of His Word to your life:

Blessed is the one who does not walk in step with the wicked or stand in the way that sinners take or sit in the company of mockers, but whose delight is in the law of the LORD, and who meditates on his law day and night. That person is like a tree planted by streams of water, which yields its fruit in season and whose leaf does not wither—whatever they do prospers.
(Ps. 1:1–3, NIV)

Please take the time to SOAP through our Bible studies and see for yourself how much more you get from your daily reading.

You'll be amazed.

SOAP STUDY *(CONTINUED)*

WHAT DOES SOAP MEAN?

S STANDS FOR
SCRIPTURE

*Physically write out the
verses.*

*You'll be amazed at what
God will reveal to you
just by taking the time to
slow down and write out
what you are reading!*

MONDAY

READ
Colossians 1:5–8

SOAP
Colossians 1:5–8

Scripture

WRITE
OUT THE
SCRIPTURE
PASSAGE
FOR THE
DAY

The faith and love that spring from the hope stored up
for you in heaven and about which you have already
heard in the true message of the gospel that has come
to you. In the same way, the gospel is bearing fruit and
growing throughout the whole world just as it has been
doing among you since the day you heard it and truly
understood God's grace. You learned it from Epaphras, our
dear fellow servant, who is a faithful minister of Christ
on our behalf, and who also told us of your love in the
Spirit.

Observations

WRITE
DOWN 1 OR 2
OBSERVATIONS
FROM THE
PASSAGE.

When you combine faith and love, you get hope. We
must remember that our hope is in heaven; it is yet to
come. The gospel is the Word of truth. The gospel is
continually bearing fruit and growing from the first day
to the last. It just takes one person to change a whole
community. Epaphras

O STANDS FOR
OBSERVATION

*What do you see in
the verses that you're
reading?*

*Who is the intended
audience? Is there a
repetition of words?*

*What words stand out
to you?*

A STANDS FOR **APPLICATION**

This is when God's Word becomes personal.

What is God saying to you today?

How can you apply what you just read to your own personal life?

What changes do you need to make? Is there action you need to take?

God used one man, Epaphras, to change a whole town. I was reminded that we are simply called to tell others about Christ; it's God's job to spread the gospel, to grow it, and have it bear fruit. I felt today's verses were almost directly spoken to Love God Greatly women: "The gospel is bearing fruit and growing throughout the whole world just as it has been doing among you since the day you heard it and truly understood God's grace.

"Dear Lord, please help me to be an Epaphras, to tell others about You and then leave the results in Your loving hands. Please help me to understand and apply personally what I have read today to my life, thereby becoming more and more like You each and every day. Help me to live a life that bears the fruit of faith and love, anchoring my hope in heaven, not here on earth. Help me to remember that the best is yet to come!

P STANDS FOR **PRAYER**

Pray God's Word back to Him. Spend time thanking Him.

If He has revealed something to you during this time in His Word, pray about it.

If He has revealed some sin that is in your life, confess. And remember, He loves you dearly.

A RECIPE FOR YOU

STOOFPEREN, DUTCH STYLE

Ingredients

2 lbs small stewing pears

a piece of lemon rind with some cloves inserted

2 cinnamon sticks

2 tbsp of dark brown sugar

1 cup of red wine

½ cup of black currant liqueur or juice (also known as Crème de Cassis)

Directions

- Peel the pears and leave whole or cut into quarters.

- Put all the ingredients in a wide pot and add additional water as needed so the liquid in the pot just covers the pears. Bring to a boil, cover with a tight-fitting lid, then reduce heat to the lowest setting possible. Leave to simmer for two to four hours (VERY GENTLY). They will have turned a deep cinnamon red when done.

- Served at room temperature with roast meats or chicken, or delicious as a dessert with vanilla ice cream! Or in a cake on top instead of apples, or on a typical Dutch pancake.

DUTCH PANCAKES

Yield: 7 to 8 pancakes

INGREDIENTS

Pancake Batter

2 cups flour (all white or any blend you like)

2 cups + 2 tbsp milk

2 large eggs

1/2 tsp salt

Fruity Variations

Stewed pears, Sliced Apples (e.g. Granny Smith), Sliced Banana, Blueberry, Topped with Strawberry and Whipped Cream

Savory Variations

Grated Sharp Cheese (e.g. Old Amsterdam, Aged Gouda or Cheddar), Bacon (cooked and chopped), Broccoli (steamed and chopped), Ham, Spinach

DIRECTIONS

For the batter:
- Combine the flour and salt.
- Mix the eggs into the flour.
- Add milk slowly (about 1/2 cup at a time) while mixing, getting rid of any lumps in the batter.

For each plain pancake:
- Lightly coat frying pan (non-stick or seasoned skillet) with sunflower oil over medium-high heat.
- Ladle 1/2 cup of batter into frying pan, coating the bottom evenly.
- Flip the pancake once all batter solidifies and brown the other side (~15-30 seconds).

Notes
- With the exception of cheese, if you're adding fruit or other ingredients, add them immediately after ladling the batter into the pan. When adding cheese, add as the batter starts to solidify.
- For savory pancakes (dinner or lunch) experiment with combinations of ham and cheese, bacon and cheese, broccoli or spinach with cheese, or create your own.
- For dessert pancakes, top plain pancakes with fruit and whipped cream or chocolate sauce.
- Top cooked pancake with some confectioner's sugar and/or (maple) syrup.

LGG DUTCH TESTIMONY

CHARISSA SCHOUTEN, NETHERLANDS

God spoke to me and freed me from so many more things I was bound by.

My name is Charissa Schouten. I am 30 years old, married for almost 10 years and the mother of three young children. I'm a busy young mom with a desire for Gods Word and helping other women grow in their faith.

I have known Jesus ever since I was little. I've known Him, known He loved me and I really felt loved by Him. I loved all the stories from the Bible. I love songs and singing about Jesus and my faith in Him. And I always felt the desire to share these stories and songs with people as a way to share my love for Jesus, but most of the time I felt unable to talk about the thing that was most important to me.

Dutch people are not used to telling their own stories, sharing their heart, their emotions, or what God has done in their lives. Like most people, we are afraid to be rejected or laughed at. We say, "Just act normal, that's weird enough!" But we love stories from other people, and with all the world news, real lives are what gets our attention.

When sharing God's Word and doing Bible studies together, I experienced a lack of personal stories. We shared knowledge, what God shows in His Word, and what the correct explanations are. But what God speaks to my heart? That is a lot more difficult.

I have been a mentor in an online program for women to help them in their marriage. That's where I shared my story and where I realized the importance of having someone to share your journey with. When that ministry ended, I came in contact with Love God Greatly via YouVersion when I followed a reading plan called "Made for Community." The personal stories and the way the women of Love God Greatly wrote spoke to my heart. So, I joined an international study group on Facebook, even though I'd never had Facebook before. I was moved by the fact that everyone was able to share her own walk with God, encouraged and cheered on by those around her, without any condemnation.

Together we studied Galatians. I knew this letter. I knew what it meant. But God spoke to me and freed me from so many more things I was bound by. I experience this freedom still every day. And now I want to share this way of doing Bible study with other women in my country. We need to learn to speak out and share what God is doing in our lives so we can encourage each other instead of keeping His riches for ourselves. I love how easily accessible and diverse the materials from Love God Greatly are. I started a group with friends and just one study later we formed two groups because we'd grown so much! Right now, in my own church, we do studies together with women ranging in age from 16 to 80! How amazing is that! We all have a platform to ask questions, share our story, share our troubles, learn from each other, and share our wisdom. I love watching as we grow in communion, in our faith, and in our relationship with Christ.

What I find so amazing about the Love God Greatly materials is that women from every denomination, every age and every part of life can share what they think and feel, and there is no condemnation. Everything you share is okay because it's your personal walk with God. You share how God is speaking to your heart and you are encouraged by the way others walk with God. This way of doing Bible study draws us out of our comfort zones, and it challenges us to engage with each other, and especially with God, every day. And then He can work in our lives when we seek Him every day and let His Spirit work in our lives. That is my desire, that through translating and facilitating I will be able to work in God's Kingdom and help others grow in their daily walk with Christ.

SINEKE VAN HEERDE, NETHERLANDS

I deeply enjoy the studies from Love God Greatly. It's just awesome to read God's Word, and these studies help me to take a closer look at specific Scripture. Sometimes I think there is not that much to learn anymore, but then I discover more treasures hidden beneath the surface of the text. I'm used to having quiet time with God, and over the years there have been so many moments that I wished I could share what I received. These studies give me that opportunity, and by sharing, I receive new insights from others as well. It's like a little window into what God is doing in the lives of others.

ADA LAMMERSE, NETHERLANDS

When Charissa told me she needed translators for Love God Greatly, I was glad to apply. By doing this, I can be of use for God and my sisters in Christ, even though I am already 76. I find it so beautiful to do work for a ministry that is focused on encouraging and equipping women in their faith and walk with the Lord so that we can grow in our own faith and be of use for the people around us. It is so good to share our stories, our thoughts, and the things God teaches us. Being able to share these studies with women in our own language is so important. It is amazing to be able to do my part in working for the Church of God through this worldwide ministry.

It is so good to share our stories, our thoughts, and the things God teaches us.

To connect with LGG Dutch Branch:

- lovegodgreatly-nederlands.blogspot.nl
- facebook.com/LGGNL

Do you know someone who could use our *Love God Greatly* Bible studies in Dutch? If so, make sure and tell them about LGG Dutch and all the amazing Bible study resources we provide to help equip them with God's Word!!!

TRUTH OVER LIES

Let's Begin

INTRODUCTION
TRUTH OVER LIES

Friend, this study we are about to embark on is for you and for me. It's for our mothers, daughters, and sisters. As well as our friends down the street and around the corner. As women there is one thing I know: we all struggle with believing lies. Lies that infiltrate our lives and aim to steal our joy.

From the moment we wake up, we struggle with the onset of lies filling our minds. And if we are not careful, we can begin to listen to those lies and worse yet, believe them.

But it doesn't have to be that way.

It's why knowing God's Word and daily renew our minds with His unchanging Truth is so important.

"Do not be conformed to this world, but be transformed by the renewal of your mind, that by testing you may discern what is the will of God, what is good and acceptable and perfect." Romans 12:2

So, friends, I invite you to join me on this journey, in this battle of fighting against lies and discovering the beautiful Truth found in God's Word. Truth that will set our hearts and minds free. Free to love who we are because of Christ and free to embrace the love He has for us.

Freedom is found in truth.

Bondage is found in lies.

Every day we are given a choice, and that choice affects the type of day we will have. Each day we have a choice to believe the lies that are spoken to us, about us or in us, or we have the choice to believe what God says and embrace the love and truth He graciously extends.

My prayer is that each of us will grow in wisdom these next six weeks and learn to be women who recognize a lie and stop it in its tracks, that we will learn to be women who speak truth over those lies.

I seriously can't wait to begin this study with you! The lies we will be covering are all lies which YOU, as our community of beautiful women, shared in our yearly survey! Lies that you said you hear, and lies which you struggle not to believe about yourself or believe about God.

These lies are what you've been battling, and as I read them, I found myself nodding and saying, "me too." I struggle with the same ones. You are not alone.

I pray each of us will walk away from this six-week study stronger and more confident in who we are and in the grace and love of our amazing heavenly Father.

And who knows, there might even be a little swagger in our step now.

READING PLAN

WEEK 1
WHO IS SPEAKING
THESE LIES & WHY?

Monday - Satan Tries to Deceive Us
Read: Genesis 3:1-4; John 8:44; Ephesians 6:11
SOAP: John 8:44; Ephesians 6:11

Tuesday - Satan Hates God & His People
Read: Acts 13:10; Revelation 12:10; 2 Thessalonians 3:3
SOAP: Revelation 12:10; 2 Thessalonians 3:3

Wednesday - We Can Deceive Ourselves
Read: Jeremiah 17:9-10; 1 Corinthians 3:18; Ezekiel 36:26
SOAP: Jeremiah 17:9-10

Thursday - We Can Be Deceived by Loving the World
Read: 1 John 5:19; 1 John 2:15-16; Colossians 2:8; 2 Timothy 3:13-14
SOAP: Colossians 2:8

Friday - We Can Be Deceived Through Our Ignorance
Read: 1 John 4:1; 1 Thessalonians 5:21; Acts 17:11; Psalm 119:11; Titus 3:3-6; James 1:22
SOAP: Psalm 119:11

WEEK 2
LIES ABOUT GOD

Monday - You Have to Earn God's Love
Read: Ephesians 2:8; 1 John 4:19
SOAP: Ephesians 2:8

Tuesday - God is Not Enough
Read: Philippians 4:19; Psalm 73:23-26; 2 Corinthians 12:9
SOAP: Philippians 4:19; 2 Corinthians 12:9

Wednesday - God Puts Shame and Guilt on You as Punishment
Read: Isaiah 54:4-5; Romans 8:1
SOAP: Romans 8:1

Thursday - God is Stingy
Read: Romans 8:31-32; John 1:16; James 1:5; Ephesians 1:3-8
SOAP: Romans 8:31-32

Friday - God Won't Forgive You for That...
Read: Isaiah 43:25; 1 John 1:9
SOAP: Isaiah 43:25; 1 John 1:9

LIES ABOUT YOU (PART 1)

Monday - You Are Not Enough
Read: Exodus 3:1-14; Exodus 4:1-11; 1 Peter 2:9; Philippians 4:13; Ephesians 2:10
SOAP: Exodus 4:11

Tuesday - You Can't Change
Read: Hebrews 13:20-21; Philippians 4:13
SOAP: Hebrews 13:20-21

Wednesday - You Aren't Loved
Read: Romans 8:37-39; Romans 5:8
SOAP: Romans 5:8

Thursday - You Need to Rely on Your Own Strength
Read: 1 Corinthians 1:26-31; Proverbs 3:5-6; Isaiah 40:28-31; Jeremiah 17:5-8
SOAP: Proverbs 3:5-6

Friday - You're Too Old/Young to be Used by God
Read: Job 12:12; Psalm 92:12-14; 1 Timothy 4:12
SOAP: Psalm 92:12-14; 1 Timothy 4:12

LIES ABOUT YOU (PART 2)

Monday - My Life is About Me
Read: Isaiah 43:1-7; Matthew 5:16; 1 Corinthians 10:31
SOAP: Isaiah 43:7

Tuesday - My Failure Defines Me
Read: 2 Corinthians 12:9-10; 1 Peter 2:9-10
SOAP: 1 Peter 2:9-10

Wednesday - My Success Defines Me
Read: Proverbs 16:18; John 15:5; James 1:17
SOAP: John 15:5

Thursday - I Can't be Confident in
the Things God has Called Me to Do
Read: 2 Corinthians 3:4-5
SOAP: 2 Corinthians 3:4-5

Friday - I Am a Victim
Read: Genesis 50:19-21; 1 Peter 2:22-23; Philippians 1:12-14;
Psalms 10:14; Isaiah 43:18-19
SOAP: Isaiah 43:18-19

LIES ABOUT HAPPINESS

Monday - Money Brings Happiness
Read: Ecclesiastes 5:10; Hebrews 13:5
SOAP: Hebrews 13:5

Tuesday - Possessions Bring Happiness
Read: Matthew 6:19-21; Luke 12:15; Ecclesiastes 3:11
SOAP: Matthew 6:19-21

Wednesday - Beauty & Health Bring Happiness
Read: 2 Corinthians 4:16-18; Proverbs 31:30; Psalm 39:4
SOAP: 2 Corinthians 4:16-18

Thursday - Happiness Can Not Be Found in Trials
Read: James 1:2-4,12; Romans 5:3-5; 1 Peter 4:12-13
SOAP: James 1:2-4

Friday - Happiness Can Be Found Apart from God
Read: Psalm 144:15; Psalm 68:3; Psalm 146:5; Psalm 4:6-7; Hebrews 1:9
SOAP: Psalm 4:6-7

WEEK 6

OVERCOMING THE LIES

Monday - Arm Yourself
Read: Ephesians 6:11-17
SOAP: Ephesians 6:11

Tuesday - Learn Wisdom
Read: Proverbs 13:20; James 1:5
SOAP: James 1:5

Wednesday - Walk in Truth
Read: John 8:31-32; John 17:17
SOAP: John 8:31-32

Thursday - Pray for Discernment
Read: Psalm 25:5; Psalm 119:6
SOAP: Psalm 25:5

Friday - Think on What is True
Read: Romans 12:2; Philippians 4:8
SOAP: Philippians 4:8

YOUR GOALS

We believe it's important to write out goals for this study. Take some time now and write three goals you would like to focus on as you begin to rise each day and dig into God's Word. Make sure and refer back to these goals throughout the next weeks to help you stay focused. You can do it!

1.

2.

3.

Signature:

Date:

WEEK 1

See to it that no one takes you captive by philosophy and empty deceit, according to human tradition, according to the elemental spirits of the world, and not according to Christ.

COLOSSIANS 2:8

PRAYER

Prayer focus for this week:
Spend time praying for your family members.

MONDAY

TUESDAY

WEDNESDAY

THURSDAY

FRIDAY

CHALLENGE

You can find this listed in our Monday blog post.

MONDAY
Scripture for Week 1

Genesis 3:1-4
1 Now the serpent was more crafty than any other beast of the field that the Lord God had made.

He said to the woman, "Did God actually say, 'You shall not eat of any tree in the garden'?" 2 And the woman said to the serpent, "We may eat of the fruit of the trees in the garden, 3 but God said, 'You shall not eat of the fruit of the tree that is in the midst of the garden, neither shall you touch it, lest you die.'" 4 But the serpent said to the woman, "You will not surely die.

John 8:44
44 You are of your father the devil, and your will is to do your father's desires. He was a murderer from the beginning, and does not stand in the truth, because there is no truth in him. When he lies, he speaks out of his own character, for he is a liar and the father of lies.

Ephesians 6:11
11 Put on the whole armor of God, that you may be able to stand against the schemes of the devil.

MONDAY

READ:
Genesis 3:1-4; John 8:44; Ephesians 6:11

SOAP:
John 8:44; Ephesians 6:11

Scripture

WRITE
OUT THE
SCRIPTURE
PASSAGE
FOR THE
DAY.

Observations

WRITE
DOWN 1 OR 2
OBSERVATIONS
FROM THE
PASSAGE.

Applications

WRITE
DOWN 1 OR 2
APPLICATIONS
FROM THE
PASSAGE.

Pray

WRITE OUT
A PRAYER
OVER WHAT
YOU LEARNED
FROM TODAY'S
PASSAGE.

TUESDAY
Scripture for Week 1

Acts 13:10
10 and said, "You son of the devil, you enemy of all righteousness, full of all deceit and villainy, will you not stop making crooked the straight paths of the Lord?

Revelation 12:10
10 And I heard a loud voice in heaven, saying, "Now the salvation and the power and the kingdom of our God and the authority of his Christ have come, for the accuser of our brothers has been thrown down, who accuses them day and night before our God.

2 Thessalonians 3:3
3 But the Lord is faithful. He will establish you and guard you against the evil one.

TUESDAY

READ:
Acts 13:10; Revelation 12:10; 2 Thessalonians 3:3

SOAP:
Revelation 12:10; 2 Thessalonians 3:3

Scripture

WRITE
OUT THE
SCRIPTURE
PASSAGE
FOR THE
DAY.

Observations

WRITE
DOWN 1 OR 2
OBSERVATIONS
FROM THE
PASSAGE.

Applications

WRITE
DOWN 1 OR 2
APPLICATIONS
FROM THE
PASSAGE.

Pray

WRITE OUT
A PRAYER
OVER WHAT
YOU LEARNED
FROM TODAY'S
PASSAGE.

WEDNESDAY

Jeremiah 17:9-10

9 The heart is deceitful above all things,
   and desperately sick;
   who can understand it?
10 "I the Lord search the heart
   and test the mind,
to give every man according to his ways,
   according to the fruit of his deeds."

1 Corinthians 3:18

18 Let no one deceive himself. If anyone among you thinks that he
is wise in this age, let him become a fool that he may become wise.

Ezekiel 36:26

26 And I will give you a new heart, and a new spirit I will put
within you. And I will remove the heart of stone from your flesh
and give you a heart of flesh.

WEDNESDAY

Scripture

WRITE
OUT THE
SCRIPTURE
PASSAGE
FOR THE
DAY.

Observations

WRITE
DOWN 1 OR 2
OBSERVATIONS
FROM THE
PASSAGE.

Applications

WRITE
DOWN 1 OR 2
APPLICATIONS
FROM THE
PASSAGE.

Pray

WRITE OUT
A PRAYER
OVER WHAT
YOU LEARNED
FROM TODAY'S
PASSAGE.

THURSDAY
Scripture for Week 1

1 John 5:19
19 We know that we are from God, and the whole world lies in the power of the evil one.

1 John 2:15-16
15 Do not love the world or the things in the world. If anyone loves the world, the love of the Father is not in him. 16 For all that is in the world—the desires of the flesh and the desires of the eyes and pride of life—is not from the Father but is from the world.

Colossians 2:8
8 See to it that no one takes you captive by philosophy and empty deceit, according to human tradition, according to the elemental spirits of the world, and not according to Christ.

2 Timothy 3:13-14
13 while evil people and impostors will go on from bad to worse, deceiving and being deceived. 14 But as for you, continue in what you have learned and have firmly believed, knowing from whom you learned it

THURSDAY

READ:
*1 John 5:19; 1 John 2:15-16; Colossians 2:8;
2 Timothy 3:13-14*

SOAP:
Colossians 2:8

Scripture

WRITE
OUT THE
SCRIPTURE
PASSAGE
FOR THE
DAY.

Observations

WRITE
DOWN 1 OR 2
OBSERVATIONS
FROM THE
PASSAGE.

Applications

WRITE
DOWN 1 OR 2
APPLICATIONS
FROM THE
PASSAGE.

Pray

WRITE OUT
A PRAYER
OVER WHAT
YOU LEARNED
FROM TODAY'S
PASSAGE.

FRIDAY

Scripture for Week 1

1 John 4:1

1 Beloved, do not believe every spirit, but test the spirits to see whether they are from God, for many false prophets have gone out into the world.

1 Thessalonians 5:21

21 but test everything; hold fast what is good.

Acts 17:11

11 Now these Jews were more noble than those in Thessalonica; they received the word with all eagerness, examining the Scriptures daily to see if these things were so.

Psalm 119:11

11 I have stored up your word in my heart,
    that I might not sin against you.

Titus 3:3-6

3 For we ourselves were once foolish, disobedient, led astray, slaves to various passions and pleasures, passing our days in malice and envy, hated by others and hating one another. 4 But when the goodness and loving kindness of God our Savior appeared, 5 he saved us, not because of works done by us in righteousness, but according to his own mercy, by the washing of regeneration and renewal of the Holy Spirit, 6 whom he poured out on us richly through Jesus Christ our Savior,

James 1:22

22 But be doers of the word, and not hearers only, deceiving yourselves.

FRIDAY

READ:
1 John 4:1; 1 Thessalonians 5:21; Acts 17:11;
Psalm 119:11; Titus 3:3-6; James 1:22

SOAP:
Psalm 119:11

Scripture

WRITE
OUT THE
SCRIPTURE
PASSAGE
FOR THE
DAY.

Observations

WRITE
DOWN 1 OR 2
OBSERVATIONS
FROM THE
PASSAGE.

Applications

WRITE
DOWN 1 OR 2
APPLICATIONS
FROM THE
PASSAGE.

Pray

WRITE OUT
A PRAYER
OVER WHAT
YOU LEARNED
FROM TODAY'S
PASSAGE.

REFLECTION
QUESTIONS

1. Why is it important to know that Satan is the father of lies?

2. Why does Satan hate God and God's people so much?

3. Why is it dangerous to follow our heart?

4. How can ignorance deceive us? What should we do about it?

5. In what ways does the world lie to us? How can we protect ourselves against those lies?

NOTES

WEEK 2

Lies About God

For of His fullness we have all received, grace upon grace.

JOHN 1:16

PRAYER

Prayer focus for this week:
Spend time praying for your country.

MONDAY

TUESDAY

WEDNESDAY

THURSDAY

FRIDAY

CHALLENGE

You can find this listed in our Monday blog post.

MONDAY
Scripture for Week 2

Ephesians 2:8
8 For by grace you have been saved through faith. And this is not your own doing; it is the gift of God,

1 John 4:19
19 We love because he first loved us.

MONDAY

READ:
Ephesians 2:8; 1 John 4:19

SOAP:
Ephesians 2:8

Scripture

WRITE
OUT THE
SCRIPTURE
PASSAGE
FOR THE
DAY.

Observations

WRITE
DOWN 1 OR 2
OBSERVATIONS
FROM THE
PASSAGE.

Applications

WRITE
DOWN 1 OR 2
APPLICATIONS
FROM THE
PASSAGE.

Pray

WRITE OUT
A PRAYER
OVER WHAT
YOU LEARNED
FROM TODAY'S
PASSAGE.

TUESDAY

Scripture for Week 2

Philippians 4:19
19 And my God will supply every need of yours according to his riches in glory in Christ Jesus.

Psalm 73:23-26
23 Nevertheless, I am continually with you;
   you hold my right hand.
24 You guide me with your counsel,
   and afterward you will receive me to glory.
25 Whom have I in heaven but you?
   And there is nothing on earth that I desire besides you.
26 My flesh and my heart may fail,
   but God is the strength of my heart and my portion forever.

2 Corinthians 12:9
9 But he said to me, "My grace is sufficient for you, for my power is made perfect in weakness." Therefore I will boast all the more gladly of my weaknesses, so that the power of Christ may rest upon me.

TUESDAY

READ:
Philippians 4:19; Psalm 73:23-26; 2 Corinthians 12:9

SOAP:
Philippians 4:19; 2 Corinthians 12:9

Scripture

WRITE
OUT THE
SCRIPTURE
PASSAGE
FOR THE
DAY.

Observations

WRITE
DOWN 1 OR 2
OBSERVATIONS
FROM THE
PASSAGE.

Applications

WRITE
DOWN 1 OR 2
APPLICATIONS
FROM THE
PASSAGE.

Pray

WRITE OUT
A PRAYER
OVER WHAT
YOU LEARNED
FROM TODAY'S
PASSAGE.

WEDNESDAY
Scripture for Week 2

Isaiah 54:4-5
4 "Fear not, for you will not be ashamed;
   be not confounded, for you will not be disgraced;
for you will forget the shame of your youth,
   and the reproach of your widowhood you will remember no
more.
5 For your Maker is your husband,
   the Lord of hosts is his name;
and the Holy One of Israel is your Redeemer,
   the God of the whole earth he is called.

Romans 8:1
1 There is therefore now no condemnation for those who are in
Christ Jesus.

WEDNESDAY

READ:
Isaiah 54:4-5; Romans 8:1

SOAP:
Romans 8:1

Scripture

WRITE
OUT THE
SCRIPTURE
PASSAGE
FOR THE
DAY.

Observations

WRITE
DOWN 1 OR 2
OBSERVATIONS
FROM THE
PASSAGE.

Applications

WRITE
DOWN 1 OR 2
APPLICATIONS
FROM THE
PASSAGE.

Pray

WRITE OUT
A PRAYER
OVER WHAT
YOU LEARNED
FROM TODAY'S
PASSAGE.

THURSDAY

Scripture for Week 2

Romans 8:31-32
31 What then shall we say to these things? If God is for us, who can be against us? 32 He who did not spare his own Son but gave him up for us all, how will he not also with him graciously give us all things?

John 1:16
16 For from his fullness we have all received, grace upon grace.

James 1:5
5 If any of you lacks wisdom, let him ask God, who gives generously to all without reproach, and it will be given him.

Ephesians 1:3-8
3 Blessed be the God and Father of our Lord Jesus Christ, who has blessed us in Christ with every spiritual blessing in the heavenly places, 4 even as he chose us in him before the foundation of the world, that we should be holy and blameless before him. In love 5 he predestined us for adoption to himself as sons through Jesus Christ, according to the purpose of his will,6 to the praise of his glorious grace, with which he has blessed us in the Beloved. 7 In him we have redemption through his blood, the forgiveness of our trespasses, according to the riches of his grace, 8 which he lavished upon us, in all wisdom and insight

THURSDAY

READ:
Romans 8:31-32; John 1:16; James 1:5; Ephesians 1:3-8

SOAP:
Romans 8:31-32

Scripture

WRITE
OUT THE
SCRIPTURE
PASSAGE
FOR THE
DAY.

Observations

WRITE
DOWN 1 OR 2
OBSERVATIONS
FROM THE
PASSAGE.

Applications

WRITE
DOWN 1 OR 2
APPLICATIONS
FROM THE
PASSAGE.

Pray

WRITE OUT
A PRAYER
OVER WHAT
YOU LEARNED
FROM TODAY'S
PASSAGE.

FRIDAY
Scripture for Week 2

Isaiah 43:25
25 "I, I am he
    who blots out your transgressions for my own sake,
    and I will not remember your sins.

1 John 1:9
9 If we confess our sins, he is faithful and just to forgive us our sins
and to cleanse us from all unrighteousness.

FRIDAY

READ:
Isaiah 43:25; 1 John 1:9

SOAP:
Isaiah 43:25; 1 John 1:9

Scripture

WRITE
OUT THE
SCRIPTURE
PASSAGE
FOR THE
DAY.

Observations

WRITE
DOWN 1 OR 2
OBSERVATIONS
FROM THE
PASSAGE.

Applications

WRITE
DOWN 1 OR 2
APPLICATIONS
FROM THE
PASSAGE.

Pray

WRITE OUT
A PRAYER
OVER WHAT
YOU LEARNED
FROM TODAY'S
PASSAGE.

REFLECTION
QUESTIONS

1. Why can't you earn God's love? How is that truth freeing?

2. Who received our shame and guilt? How should that change us?

3. In what ways do we believe the lie that God is not enough? What is the truth?

4. Does God forgive all of our sins? Is any sin bigger than God's sacrifice and mercy?

5. What causes us to believe that God is not generous? Can you see God's generosity in your life? In what ways?

NOTES

WEEK 3

Lies About You (Part 1)

Let no one despise you for your youth,

but set the believers an example

in speech, in conduct, in love,

in faith, in purity.

1 TIMOTHY 4:12

PRAYER

Prayer focus for this week:
Spend time praying for your friends.

MONDAY

TUESDAY

WEDNESDAY

THURSDAY

FRIDAY

CHALLENGE

You can find this listed in our Monday blog post.

MONDAY

Exodus 3:1-14

1 Now Moses was keeping the flock of his father-in-law, Jethro, the priest of Midian, and he led his flock to the west side of the wilderness and came to Horeb, the mountain of God. 2 And the angel of the Lord appeared to him in a flame of fire out of the midst of a bush. He looked, and behold, the bush was burning, yet it was not consumed. 3 And Moses said, "I will turn aside to see this great sight, why the bush is not burned." 4 When the Lord saw that he turned aside to see, God called to him out of the bush, "Moses, Moses!" And he said, "Here I am." 5 Then he said, "Do not come near; take your sandals off your feet, for the place on which you are standing is holy ground." 6 And he said, "I am the God of your father, the God of Abraham, the God of Isaac, and the God of Jacob." And Moses hid his face, for he was afraid to look at God.

7 Then the Lord said, "I have surely seen the affliction of my people who are in Egypt and have heard their cry because of their taskmasters. I know their sufferings, 8 and I have come down to deliver them out of the hand of the Egyptians and to bring them up out of that land to a good and broad land, a land flowing with milk and honey, to the place of the Canaanites, the Hittites, the Amorites, the Perizzites, the Hivites, and the Jebusites. 9 And now, behold, the cry of the people of Israel has come to me, and I have also seen the oppression with which the Egyptians oppress them. 10 Come, I will send you to Pharaoh that you may bring my people, the children of Israel, out of Egypt." 11 But Moses said to God, "Who am I that I should go to Pharaoh and bring the children of Israel out of Egypt?" 12 He said, "But I will be with you, and this shall be the sign for you, that I have sent you: when you have brought the people out of Egypt, you shall serve God on this mountain."

13 Then Moses said to God, "If I come to the people of Israel and say to them, 'The God of your fathers has sent me to you,' and they ask me, 'What is his name?' what shall I say to them?" 14 God said to Moses, "I am who I am." And he said, "Say this to the people of Israel: 'I am has sent me to you.'"

Exodus 4:1-11

1 Then Moses answered, "But behold, they will not believe me or listen to my voice, for they will say, 'The Lord did not appear to you.'" 2 The Lord said to him, "What is that in your hand?" He said, "A staff." 3 And he said, "Throw it on the ground." So he threw it on the ground, and it became a serpent, and Moses ran from it. 4 But the Lord said to Moses, "Put out your hand and catch it by the tail"—so he put out his hand and caught it, and it became a staff in his hand— 5 "that they may believe that the Lord, the God of their fathers, the God of Abraham, the God of Isaac, and the God of Jacob, has appeared to you." 6 Again, the Lord said to him, "Put your hand inside your cloak." And he put his hand inside his cloak, and when he took it out, behold, his hand was leprous like snow. 7 Then God said, "Put your hand back inside your cloak." So he put his hand back inside his cloak, and when he took it out, behold, it was restored like the rest of his flesh. 8 "If they will not believe you," God said, "or listen to the first sign, they may believe the latter sign. 9 If they will not believe even these two signs or listen to your voice, you shall take some water from the Nile and pour it on the dry ground, and the water that you shall take from the Nile will become blood on the dry ground."

10 But Moses said to the Lord, "Oh, my Lord, I am not eloquent, either in the past or since you have spoken to your servant, but I am slow of speech and of tongue." 11 Then the Lord said to him, "Who has made man's mouth? Who makes him mute, or deaf, or seeing, or blind? Is it not I, the Lord?

1 Peter 2:9

9 But you are a chosen race, a royal priesthood, a holy nation, a people for his own possession, that you may proclaim the excellencies of him who called you out of darkness into his marvelous light.

Philippians 4:13

13 I can do all things through him who strengthens me.

Ephesians 2:10

10 For we are his workmanship, created in Christ Jesus for good works, which God prepared beforehand, that we should walk in them.

MONDAY

READ:
*Exodus 3:1-14; Exodus 4:1-11; 1 Peter 2:9;
Philippians 4:13; Ephesians 2:10*

SOAP:
Exodus 4:11

Scripture

WRITE
OUT THE
SCRIPTURE
PASSAGE
FOR THE
DAY.

Observations

WRITE
DOWN 1 OR 2
OBSERVATIONS
FROM THE
PASSAGE.

Applications

WRITE
DOWN 1 OR 2
APPLICATIONS
FROM THE
PASSAGE.

Pray

WRITE OUT
A PRAYER
OVER WHAT
YOU LEARNED
FROM TODAY'S
PASSAGE.

TUESDAY
Scripture for Week 3

Hebrews 13:20-21
20 Now may the God of peace who brought again from the dead
our Lord Jesus, the great shepherd of the sheep, by the blood of
the eternal covenant, 21 equip you with everything good that you
may do his will, working in us that which is pleasing in his sight,
through Jesus Christ, to whom be glory forever and ever. Amen.

Philippians 4:13
13 I can do all things through him who strengthens me.

TUESDAY

READ:
Hebrews 13:20-21; Philippians 4:13

SOAP:
Hebrews 13:20-21

Scripture

WRITE
OUT THE
SCRIPTURE
PASSAGE
FOR THE
DAY.

Observations

WRITE
DOWN 1 OR 2
OBSERVATIONS
FROM THE
PASSAGE.

Applications

WRITE
DOWN 1 OR 2
APPLICATIONS
FROM THE
PASSAGE.

Pray

WRITE OUT
A PRAYER
OVER WHAT
YOU LEARNED
FROM TODAY'S
PASSAGE.

WEDNESDAY
Scripture for Week 3

Romans 8:37-39
37 No, in all these things we are more than conquerors through him who loved us. 38 For I am sure that neither death nor life, nor angels nor rulers, nor things present nor things to come, nor powers, 39 nor height nor depth, nor anything else in all creation, will be able to separate us from the love of God in Christ Jesus our Lord.

Romans 5:8
8 but God shows his love for us in that while we were still sinners, Christ died for us.

WEDNESDAY

READ:
Romans 8:37-39; Romans 5:8

SOAP:
Romans 5:8

Scripture

WRITE
OUT THE
SCRIPTURE
PASSAGE
FOR THE
DAY.

Observations

WRITE
DOWN 1 OR 2
OBSERVATIONS
FROM THE
PASSAGE.

Applications

WRITE
DOWN 1 OR 2
APPLICATIONS
FROM THE
PASSAGE.

Pray

WRITE OUT
A PRAYER
OVER WHAT
YOU LEARNED
FROM TODAY'S
PASSAGE.

THURSDAY
Scripture for Week 3

1 Corinthians 1:26-31

26 For consider your calling, brothers: not many of you were wise according to worldly standards, not many were powerful, not many were of noble birth. 27 But God chose what is foolish in the world to shame the wise; God chose what is weak in the world to shame the strong; 28 God chose what is low and despised in the world, even things that are not, to bring to nothing things that are,29 so that no human being might boast in the presence of God.30 And because of him you are in Christ Jesus, who became to us wisdom from God, righteousness and sanctification and redemption, 31 so that, as it is written, "Let the one who boasts, boast in the Lord."

Proverbs 3:5-6

5 Trust in the Lord with all your heart,
    and do not lean on your own understanding.
6 In all your ways acknowledge him,
    and he will make straight your paths.

Isaiah 40:28-31

28 Have you not known? Have you not heard?
The Lord is the everlasting God,
    the Creator of the ends of the earth.
He does not faint or grow weary;
    his understanding is unsearchable.
29 He gives power to the faint,
    and to him who has no might he increases strength.
30 Even youths shall faint and be weary,
    and young men shall fall exhausted;
31 but they who wait for the Lord shall renew their strength;
    they shall mount up with wings like eagles;
they shall run and not be weary;
    they shall walk and not faint.

Jeremiah 17:5-8

5 Thus says the Lord:
"Cursed is the man who trusts in man
    and makes flesh his strength,
    whose heart turns away from the Lord.
6 He is like a shrub in the desert,
    and shall not see any good come.
He shall dwell in the parched places of the wilderness,
    in an uninhabited salt land.
7 "Blessed is the man who trusts in the Lord,
    whose trust is the Lord.
8 He is like a tree planted by water,
    that sends out its roots by the stream,
and does not fear when heat comes,
    for its leaves remain green,
and is not anxious in the year of drought,
    for it does not cease to bear fruit."

THURSDAY

READ:
*1 Corinthians 1:26-31; Proverbs 3:5-6;
Isaiah 40:28-31; Jeremiah 17:5-8*

SOAP:
Proverbs 3:5-6

Scripture

WRITE
OUT THE
SCRIPTURE
PASSAGE
FOR THE
DAY.

Observations

WRITE
DOWN 1 OR 2
OBSERVATIONS
FROM THE
PASSAGE.

Applications

WRITE
DOWN 1 OR 2
APPLICATIONS
FROM THE
PASSAGE.

Pray

WRITE OUT
A PRAYER
OVER WHAT
YOU LEARNED
FROM TODAY'S
PASSAGE.

FRIDAY
Scripture for Week 3

Job 12:12
12 Wisdom is with the aged,
   and understanding in length of days.

Psalm 92:12-14
12 The righteous flourish like the palm tree
   and grow like a cedar in Lebanon.
13 They are planted in the house of the Lord;
   they flourish in the courts of our God.
14 They still bear fruit in old age;
   they are ever full of sap and green,

1 Timothy 4:12
12 Let no one despise you for your youth, but set the believers an
example in speech, in conduct, in love, in faith, in purity.

FRIDAY

READ:
Job 12:12; Psalm 92:12-14; 1 Timothy 4:12

SOAP:
Psalm 92:12-14; 1 Timothy 4:12

Scripture

WRITE
OUT THE
SCRIPTURE
PASSAGE
FOR THE
DAY.

Observations

WRITE
DOWN 1 OR 2
OBSERVATIONS
FROM THE
PASSAGE.

Applications

WRITE
DOWN 1 OR 2
APPLICATIONS
FROM THE
PASSAGE.

Pray

WRITE OUT
A PRAYER
OVER WHAT
YOU LEARNED
FROM TODAY'S
PASSAGE.

REFLECTION QUESTIONS

1. How can we overcome feelings of inadequacy?

2. Why does relying on ourselves not produce lasting change? How does relying on Jesus bring about true change?

3. How do you know that we are loved by God?

4. What is the danger of relying on our own strength? How do we rest in God's strength?

5. Does your age make you feel inferior? How can God use the young and the old?

NOTES

WEEK 4

Lies About You (Part 2)

But he said to me, "My grace is sufficient for you, for my power is made perfect in weakness." Therefore I will boast all the more gladly of my weaknesses, so that the power of Christ may rest upon me. For the sake of Christ, then, I am content with weaknesses, insults, hardships, persecutions, and calamities. For when I am weak, then I am strong.

2 CORINTHIANS 12:9-10

PRAYER

Prayer focus for this week:
Spend time praying for your church.

MONDAY

TUESDAY

WEDNESDAY

THURSDAY

FRIDAY

CHALLENGE

You can find this listed in our Monday blog post.

86

MONDAY

Scripture for Week 4

Isaiah 43:1-7
1 But now thus says the Lord,
he who created you, O Jacob,
   he who formed you, O Israel:
"Fear not, for I have redeemed you;
   I have called you by name, you are mine.
2 When you pass through the waters, I will be with you;
   and through the rivers, they shall not overwhelm you;
when you walk through fire you shall not be burned,
   and the flame shall not consume you.
3 For I am the Lord your God,
   the Holy One of Israel, your Savior.
I give Egypt as your ransom,
   Cush and Seba in exchange for you.
4 Because you are precious in my eyes,
   and honored, and I love you,
I give men in return for you,
   peoples in exchange for your life.
5 Fear not, for I am with you;
   I will bring your offspring from the east,
   and from the west I will gather you.
6 I will say to the north, Give up,
   and to the south, Do not withhold;
bring my sons from afar
   and my daughters from the end of the earth,
7 everyone who is called by my name,
   whom I created for my glory,
   whom I formed and made."

Matthew 5:16
16 In the same way, let your light shine before others, so that they may see your good works and give glory to your Father who is in heaven.

1 Corinthians 10:31
31 So, whether you eat or drink, or whatever you do, do all to the glory of God.

MONDAY

READ:
Isaiah 43:1-7; Matthew 5:16; 1 Corinthians 10:31

SOAP:
Isaiah 43:7

Scripture

WRITE
OUT THE
SCRIPTURE
PASSAGE
FOR THE
DAY.

Observations

WRITE
DOWN 1 OR 2
OBSERVATIONS
FROM THE
PASSAGE.

Applications

WRITE
DOWN 1 OR 2
APPLICATIONS
FROM THE
PASSAGE.

Pray

WRITE OUT
A PRAYER
OVER WHAT
YOU LEARNED
FROM TODAY'S
PASSAGE.

TUESDAY
Scripture for Week 4

2 Corinthians 12:9-10
9 But he said to me, "My grace is sufficient for you, for my power is made perfect in weakness." Therefore I will boast all the more gladly of my weaknesses, so that the power of Christ may rest upon me. 10 For the sake of Christ, then, I am content with weaknesses, insults, hardships, persecutions, and calamities. For when I am weak, then I am strong.

1 Peter 2:9-10
9 But you are a chosen race, a royal priesthood, a holy nation, a people for his own possession, that you may proclaim the excellencies of him who called you out of darkness into his marvelous light. 10 Once you were not a people, but now you are God's people; once you had not received mercy, but now you have received mercy.

TUESDAY

READ:
2 Corinthians 12:9-10; 1 Peter 2:9-10

SOAP:
1 Peter 2:9-10

Scripture

WRITE
OUT THE
SCRIPTURE
PASSAGE
FOR THE
DAY.

Observations

WRITE
DOWN 1 OR 2
OBSERVATIONS
FROM THE
PASSAGE.

Applications

WRITE
DOWN 1 OR 2
APPLICATIONS
FROM THE
PASSAGE.

Pray

WRITE OUT
A PRAYER
OVER WHAT
YOU LEARNED
FROM TODAY'S
PASSAGE.

WEDNESDAY
Scripture for Week 4

Proverbs 16:18
18 Pride goes before destruction,
  and a haughty spirit before a fall.

John 15:5
5 I am the vine; you are the branches. Whoever abides in me and I in him, he it is that bears much fruit, for apart from me you can do nothing.

James 1:17
17 Every good gift and every perfect gift is from above, coming down from the Father of lights, with whom there is no variation or shadow due to change.

WEDNESDAY

READ:
Proverbs 16:18; John 15:5; James 1:17

SOAP:
John 15:5

Scripture

WRITE
OUT THE
SCRIPTURE
PASSAGE
FOR THE
DAY.

Observations

WRITE
DOWN 1 OR 2
OBSERVATIONS
FROM THE
PASSAGE.

Applications

WRITE
DOWN 1 OR 2
APPLICATIONS
FROM THE
PASSAGE.

Pray

WRITE OUT
A PRAYER
OVER WHAT
YOU LEARNED
FROM TODAY'S
PASSAGE.

THURSDAY
Scripture for Week 4

2 Corinthians 3:4-5
4 Such is the confidence that we have through Christ toward
God. 5 Not that we are sufficient in ourselves to claim anything as
coming from us, but our sufficiency is from God,

THURSDAY

READ:
2 Corinthians 3:4-5

SOAP:
2 Corinthians 3:4-5

Scripture

WRITE
OUT THE
SCRIPTURE
PASSAGE
FOR THE
DAY.

Observations

WRITE
DOWN 1 OR 2
OBSERVATIONS
FROM THE
PASSAGE.

Applications

WRITE
DOWN 1 OR 2
APPLICATIONS
FROM THE
PASSAGE.

Pray

WRITE OUT
A PRAYER
OVER WHAT
YOU LEARNED
FROM TODAY'S
PASSAGE.

FRIDAY
Scripture for Week 4

Genesis 50:19-21
19 But Joseph said to them, "Do not fear, for am I in the place of
God? 20 As for you, you meant evil against me, but God meant it
for good, to bring it about that many people should be kept alive,
as they are today. 21 So do not fear; I will provide for you and your
little ones." Thus he comforted them and spoke kindly to them.

1 Peter 2:22-23
22 He committed no sin, neither was deceit found in his
mouth.23 When he was reviled, he did not revile in return; when he
suffered, he did not threaten, but continued entrusting himself to
him who judges justly.

Philippians 1:12-14
12 I want you to know, brothers, that what has happened to me has
really served to advance the gospel, 13 so that it has become known
throughout the whole imperial guard and to all the rest that my
imprisonment is for Christ. 14 And most of the brothers, having
become confident in the Lord by my imprisonment, are much more
bold to speak the word without fear.

Psalms 10:14
14 But you do see, for you note mischief and vexation,
    that you may take it into your hands;
to you the helpless commits himself;
    you have been the helper of the fatherless.

Isaiah 43:18-19
18 "Remember not the former things,
    nor consider the things of old.
19 Behold, I am doing a new thing;
    now it springs forth, do you not perceive it?
I will make a way in the wilderness
    and rivers in the desert.

FRIDAY

READ:
Genesis 50:19-21; 1 Peter 2:22-23; Philippians 1:12-14;
Psalms 10:14; Isaiah 43:18-19

SOAP:
Isaiah 43:18-19

Scripture

WRITE
OUT THE
SCRIPTURE
PASSAGE
FOR THE
DAY.

Observations

WRITE
DOWN 1 OR 2
OBSERVATIONS
FROM THE
PASSAGE.

Applications

WRITE
DOWN 1 OR 2
APPLICATIONS
FROM THE
PASSAGE.

Pray

WRITE OUT
A PRAYER
OVER WHAT
YOU LEARNED
FROM TODAY'S
PASSAGE.

REFLECTION QUESTIONS

1. Why is it dangerous to think our lives are about us?

2. Why do we let failures get us down? How should a proper view of our identity affect the way we view our failures?

3. How should a proper view of our identity affect the way we view our successes?

4. God calls us to do many different things. Why should our confidence not be found in ourselves? In whom should we find our confidence? How will this affect our work?

5. Why is it important to see yourself the way God sees you?

NOTES

WEEK 5

Lies About Happiness

And he said to them, "Take care, and be on your guard against all covetousness, for one's life does not consist in the abundance of his possessions."

LUKE 12:15

PRAYER

Prayer focus for this week:
Spend time praying for missionaries.

MONDAY

TUESDAY

WEDNESDAY

THURSDAY

FRIDAY

CHALLENGE

You can find this listed in our Monday blog post.

MONDAY
Scripture for Week 5

Ecclesiastes 5:10
10 He who loves money will not be satisfied with money, nor he who loves wealth with his income; this also is vanity.

Hebrews 13:5
5 Keep your life free from love of money, and be content with what you have, for he has said, "I will never leave you nor forsake you."

MONDAY

READ:
Ecclesiastes 5:10; Hebrews 13:5

SOAP:
Hebrews 13:5

Scripture

WRITE
OUT THE
SCRIPTURE
PASSAGE
FOR THE
DAY.

Observations

WRITE
DOWN 1 OR 2
OBSERVATIONS
FROM THE
PASSAGE.

Applications

WRITE
DOWN 1 OR 2
APPLICATIONS
FROM THE
PASSAGE.

Pray

WRITE OUT
A PRAYER
OVER WHAT
YOU LEARNED
FROM TODAY'S
PASSAGE.

TUESDAY

Scripture for Week 5

Matthew 6:19-21
19 "Do not lay up for yourselves treasures on earth, where moth and rust destroy and where thieves break in and steal, 20 but lay up for yourselves treasures in heaven, where neither moth nor rust destroys and where thieves do not break in and steal. 21 For where your treasure is, there your heart will be also.

Luke 12:15
15 And he said to them, "Take care, and be on your guard against all covetousness, for one's life does not consist in the abundance of his possessions."

Ecclesiastes 3:11
11 He has made everything beautiful in its time. Also, he has put eternity into man's heart, yet so that he cannot find out what God has done from the beginning to the end.

TUESDAY

READ:
Matthew 6:19-21; Luke 12:15; Ecclesiastes 3:11

SOAP:
Matthew 6:19-21

Scripture

WRITE
OUT THE
SCRIPTURE
PASSAGE
FOR THE
DAY.

Observations

WRITE
DOWN 1 OR 2
OBSERVATIONS
FROM THE
PASSAGE.

Applications

WRITE
DOWN 1 OR 2
APPLICATIONS
FROM THE
PASSAGE.

Pray

WRITE OUT
A PRAYER
OVER WHAT
YOU LEARNED
FROM TODAY'S
PASSAGE.

WEDNESDAY
Scripture for Week 5

2 Corinthians 4:16-18

16 So we do not lose heart. Though our outer self is wasting away, our inner self is being renewed day by day. 17 For this light momentary affliction is preparing for us an eternal weight of glory beyond all comparison, 18 as we look not to the things that are seen but to the things that are unseen. For the things that are seen are transient, but the things that are unseen are eternal.

Proverbs 31:30

30 Charm is deceitful, and beauty is vain,
   but a woman who fears the Lord is to be praised.

Psalm 39:4

4 "O Lord, make me know my end
   and what is the measure of my days;
   let me know how fleeting I am!

WEDNESDAY

READ:
2 Corinthians 4:16-18; Proverbs 31:30; Psalm 39:4

SOAP:
2 Corinthians 4:16-18

Scripture

WRITE
OUT THE
SCRIPTURE
PASSAGE
FOR THE
DAY.

Observations

WRITE
DOWN 1 OR 2
OBSERVATIONS
FROM THE
PASSAGE.

Applications

WRITE
DOWN 1 OR 2
APPLICATIONS
FROM THE
PASSAGE.

Pray

WRITE OUT
A PRAYER
OVER WHAT
YOU LEARNED
FROM TODAY'S
PASSAGE.

THURSDAY
Scripture for Week 5

James 1:2-4,12

2 Count it all joy, my brothers, when you meet trials of various kinds, 3 for you know that the testing of your faith produces steadfastness. 4 And let steadfastness have its full effect, that you may be perfect and complete, lacking in nothing. 12 Blessed is the man who remains steadfast under trial, for when he has stood the test he will receive the crown of life, which God has promised to those who love him.

Romans 5:3-5

3 Not only that, but we rejoice in our sufferings, knowing that suffering produces endurance, 4 and endurance produces character, and character produces hope, 5 and hope does not put us to shame, because God's love has been poured into our hearts through the Holy Spirit who has been given to us.

1 Peter 4:12-13

12 Beloved, do not be surprised at the fiery trial when it comes upon you to test you, as though something strange were happening to you. 13 But rejoice insofar as you share Christ's sufferings, that you may also rejoice and be glad when his glory is revealed.

THURSDAY

READ:
James 1:2-4,12; Romans 5:3-5; 1 Peter 4:12-13

SOAP:
James 1:2-4

Scripture

WRITE
OUT THE
SCRIPTURE
PASSAGE
FOR THE
DAY.

Observations

WRITE
DOWN 1 OR 2
OBSERVATIONS
FROM THE
PASSAGE.

Applications

WRITE
DOWN 1 OR 2
APPLICATIONS
FROM THE
PASSAGE.

Pray

WRITE OUT
A PRAYER
OVER WHAT
YOU LEARNED
FROM TODAY'S
PASSAGE.

FRIDAY

Scripture for Week 5

Psalm 144:15
15 Blessed are the people to whom such blessings fall!
   Blessed are the people whose God is the Lord!

Psalm 68:3
3 But the righteous shall be glad;
   they shall exult before God;
   they shall be jubilant with joy!

Psalm 146:5
5 Blessed is he whose help is the God of Jacob,
   whose hope is in the Lord his God,

Psalm 4:6-7
6 There are many who say, "Who will show us some good?
   Lift up the light of your face upon us, O Lord!"
7 You have put more joy in my heart
   than they have when their grain and wine abound.

Hebrews 1:9
9 You have loved righteousness and hated wickedness;
therefore God, your God, has anointed you
   with the oil of gladness beyond your companions.

FRIDAY

READ:
*Psalm 144:15; Psalm 68:3; Psalm 146:5; Psalm 4:6-7;
Hebrews 1:9*

SOAP:
Psalm 4:6-7

Scripture

WRITE
OUT THE
SCRIPTURE
PASSAGE
FOR THE
DAY.

Observations

WRITE
DOWN 1 OR 2
OBSERVATIONS
FROM THE
PASSAGE.

Applications

WRITE
DOWN 1 OR 2
APPLICATIONS
FROM THE
PASSAGE.

Pray

WRITE OUT
A PRAYER
OVER WHAT
YOU LEARNED
FROM TODAY'S
PASSAGE.

REFLECTION
QUESTIONS

1. Why shouldn't we love money? What is the proper view of money?

2. Why can't possessions provide us with the happiness we long for?

3. What lies do you believe about your body and your health? What is the truth?

4. How is it possible to be joyful during hard times?

5. Can you truly be happy apart from God?

NOTES

WEEK 6

Overcoming the Lies

Guide me in your truth and teach me,

for you are God my Savior,

and my hope is in you all day long.

PSALM 25:5

PRAYER

Prayer focus for this week:
Spend time praying for yourself.

MONDAY

TUESDAY

WEDNESDAY

THURSDAY

FRIDAY

CHALLENGE

You can find this listed in our Monday blog post.

126

MONDAY
Scripture for Week 6

Ephesians 6:11-17

11 Put on the whole armor of God, that you may be able to stand against the schemes of the devil. 12 For we do not wrestle against flesh and blood, but against the rulers, against the authorities, against the cosmic powers over this present darkness, against the spiritual forces of evil in the heavenly places. 13 Therefore take up the whole armor of God, that you may be able to withstand in the evil day, and having done all, to stand firm. 14 Stand therefore, having fastened on the belt of truth, and having put on the breastplate of righteousness, 15 and, as shoes for your feet, having put on the readiness given by the gospel of peace. 16 In all circumstances take up the shield of faith, with which you can extinguish all the flaming darts of the evil one; 17 and take the helmet of salvation, and the sword of the Spirit, which is the word of God,

MONDAY

READ:
Ephesians 6:11-17

SOAP:
Ephesians 6:11

Scripture

WRITE
OUT THE
SCRIPTURE
PASSAGE
FOR THE
DAY.

Observations

WRITE
DOWN 1 OR 2
OBSERVATIONS
FROM THE
PASSAGE.

Applications

WRITE
DOWN 1 OR 2
APPLICATIONS
FROM THE
PASSAGE.

Pray

WRITE OUT
A PRAYER
OVER WHAT
YOU LEARNED
FROM TODAY'S
PASSAGE.

TUESDAY
Scripture for Week 6

Proverbs 13:20
20 Whoever walks with the wise becomes wise,
   but the companion of fools will suffer harm.

James 1:5
5 If any of you lacks wisdom, let him ask God, who gives generously
to all without reproach, and it will be given him.

TUESDAY

READ:
Proverbs 13:20; James 1:5

SOAP:
James 1:5

Scripture

WRITE
OUT THE
SCRIPTURE
PASSAGE
FOR THE
DAY.

Observations

WRITE
DOWN 1 OR 2
OBSERVATIONS
FROM THE
PASSAGE.

Applications

WRITE
DOWN 1 OR 2
APPLICATIONS
FROM THE
PASSAGE.

Pray

WRITE OUT
A PRAYER
OVER WHAT
YOU LEARNED
FROM TODAY'S
PASSAGE.

WEDNESDAY
Scripture for Week 6

John 8:31-32
31 So Jesus said to the Jews who had believed him, "If you abide in my word, you are truly my disciples, 32 and you will know the truth, and the truth will set you free."

John 17:17
17 Sanctify them in the truth; your word is truth.

WEDNESDAY

READ:
John 8:31-32; John 17:17

SOAP:
John 8:31-32

Scripture

WRITE
OUT THE
SCRIPTURE
PASSAGE
FOR THE
DAY.

Observations

WRITE
DOWN 1 OR 2
OBSERVATIONS
FROM THE
PASSAGE.

Applications

WRITE
DOWN 1 OR 2
APPLICATIONS
FROM THE
PASSAGE.

Pray

WRITE OUT
A PRAYER
OVER WHAT
YOU LEARNED
FROM TODAY'S
PASSAGE.

THURSDAY
Scripture for Week 6

Psalm 25:5
5 Lead me in your truth and teach me,
    for you are the God of my salvation;
    for you I wait all the day long.

Psalm 119:6
6 Then I shall not be put to shame,
    having my eyes fixed on all your commandments.

THURSDAY

READ:
Psalm 25:5; Psalm 119:6

SOAP:
Psalm 25:5

Scripture

WRITE
OUT THE
SCRIPTURE
PASSAGE
FOR THE
DAY.

Observations

WRITE
DOWN 1 OR 2
OBSERVATIONS
FROM THE
PASSAGE.

Applications

WRITE DOWN 1 OR 2 APPLICATIONS FROM THE PASSAGE.

Pray

WRITE OUT A PRAYER OVER WHAT YOU LEARNED FROM TODAY'S PASSAGE.

FRIDAY
Scripture for Week 6

Romans 12:2
2 Do not be conformed to this world, but be transformed by the renewal of your mind, that by testing you may discern what is the will of God, what is good and acceptable and perfect.

Philippians 4:8
8 Finally, brothers, whatever is true, whatever is honorable, whatever is just, whatever is pure, whatever is lovely, whatever is commendable, if there is any excellence, if there is anything worthy of praise, think about these things.

FRIDAY

READ:
Romans 12:2; Philippians 4:8

SOAP:
Philippians 4:8

Scripture

WRITE
OUT THE
SCRIPTURE
PASSAGE
FOR THE
DAY.

Observations

WRITE
DOWN 1 OR 2
OBSERVATIONS
FROM THE
PASSAGE.

Applications

WRITE
DOWN 1 OR 2
APPLICATIONS
FROM THE
PASSAGE.

Pray

WRITE OUT
A PRAYER
OVER WHAT
YOU LEARNED
FROM TODAY'S
PASSAGE.

REFLECTION
QUESTIONS

1. How do we need to fight the devil and his lies?

2. Why is it important to surround ourselves with people who are wise?

3. Where do we find truth and what does it mean to "walk in truth"?

4. What is discernment?

5. How does thinking on what is true help us overcome lies?

NOTES

KNOW THESE TRUTHS

from God's Word

God loves you.

Even when you're feeling unworthy and like the world is stacked against you, God loves you - yes, you - and He has created you for great purpose.

God's Word says, "God so loved the world that He gave His one and only Son, Jesus, that whoever believes in Him shall not perish, but have eternal life" (John 3:16).

Our sin separates us from God.

We are all sinners by nature and by choice, and because of this we are separated from God, who is holy.

God's Word says, "All have sinned and fall short of the glory of God" (Romans 3:23).

Jesus died so that you might have life.

The consequence of sin is death, but your story doesn't have to end there! God's free gift of salvation is available to us because Jesus took the penalty for our sin when He died on the cross.

God's Word says, "For the wages of sin is death, but the free gift of God is eternal life in Christ Jesus our Lord" (Romans 6:23); "God demonstrates His own love toward us, in that while we were yet sinners, Christ died for us" (Romans 5:8).

Jesus lives!

Death could not hold Him, and three days after His body was placed in the tomb Jesus rose again, defeating sin and death forever! He lives today in heaven and is preparing a place in eternity for all who believe in Him.

God's Word says, "In my Father's house are many rooms. If it were not so, would I have told you that I go to prepare a place for you? And if I go and prepare a place for you, I will come again and will take you to myself, that where I am you may be also" (John 14:2-3).

Yes, you can KNOW that you are forgiven.
Accept Jesus as the only way to salvation…

Accepting Jesus as your Savior is not about what you can do, but rather about having faith in what Jesus has already done. It takes recognizing that you are a sinner, believing that Jesus died for your sins, and asking for forgiveness by placing your full trust in Jesus's work on the cross on your behalf.

God's Word says, "If you confess with your mouth that Jesus is Lord and believe in your heart that God raised him from the dead, you will be saved. For with the heart one believes and is justified, and with the mouth one confesses and is saved" (Romans 10:9-10).

Practically, what does that look like?
With a sincere heart, you can pray a simple prayer like this:

God,
I know that I am a sinner.
I don't want to live another day without embracing
the love and forgiveness that You have for me.
I ask for Your forgiveness.
I believe that You died for my sins and rose from the dead.
I surrender all that I am and ask You to be Lord of my life.
Help me to turn from my sin and follow You.
Teach me what it means to walk in freedom as I live under Your grace,
and help me to grow in Your ways as I seek to know You more.
Amen.

If you just prayed this prayer (or something similar in your own words), would you email us at info@lovegodgreatly.com?

We'd love to help get you started on this exciting journey as a child of God!

WELCOME
FRIEND

We're so glad
you're here

Love God Greatly exists to inspire, encourage, and equip women all over the world to make God's Word a priority in their lives.

INSPIRE
women to make God's Word a priority in their daily lives through our Bible study resources.

ENCOURAGE
women in their daily walks with God through online community and personal accountability.

EQUIP
women to grow in their faith, so that they can effectively reach others for Christ.

Love God Greatly consists of a beautiful community of women who use a variety of technology platforms to keep each other accountable in God's Word.

We start with a simple Bible reading plan, but it doesn't stop there.

Some gather in homes and churches locally, while others connect online with women across the globe. Whatever the method, we lovingly lock arms and unite for this purpose...to Love God Greatly with our lives.

At Love God Greatly, you'll find real, authentic women. Women who are imperfect, yet forgiven. Women who desire less of us, and a whole lot more of Jesus. Women who long to know God through his Word, because we know that Truth transforms and sets us free. Women who are better together, saturated in God's Word and in community with one another.

Love God Greatly is a 501 (C) (3) non-profit organization. Funding for Love God Greatly comes through donations and proceeds from our online Bible study journals and books. LGG is committed to providing quality Bible study materials and believes finances should never get in the way of a woman being able to participate in one of our studies. All journals and translated journals are available to download for free from LoveGodGreatly.com for those who cannot afford to purchase them. Our journals and books are also available for sale on Amazon. Search for "Love God Greatly" to see all of our Bible study journals and books. 100% of proceeds go directly back into supporting Love God Greatly and helping us inspire, encourage and equip women all over the world with God's Word.

THANK YOU for partnering with us!

WHAT WE OFFER:

18 + Translations | Bible Reading Plans | Online Bible Study
Love God Greatly App | 80 + Countries Served
Bible Study Journals & Books | Community Groups

EACH LGG STUDY INCLUDES:

Three Devotional Corresponding Blog Posts
Memory Verses | Weekly Challenge | Weekly Reading Plan
Reflection Questions And More!

OTHER LOVE GOD GREATLY STUDIES INCLUDE:

Truth Over Lies | Fear & Anxiety | James | His Name Is...
Philippians | 1 & 2 Timothy | Sold Out | Ruth | Broken & Redeemed
Walking in Wisdom | God With Us | In Everything Give Thanks
You Are Forgiven | David | Ecclesiastes | Growing Through Prayer
Names of God | Galatians | Psalm 119 | 1st & 2nd Peter
Made For Community | The Road To Christmas
The Source Of Gratitude | Esther | You Are Loved

Visit us online at

LOVEGODGREATLY.COM

89496738R00086

Made in the USA
Lexington, KY
29 May 2018